PEOPLE FROM THE PIT STAND UP

PEOPLE FROM THE PIT STAND UP

SAM DUCKOR-JONES

VICTORIA UNIVERSITY PRESS

TE WHARE WĀNANGA O TE ŪPOKO O TE IKA A MĀUI

VICTORIA
UNIVERSITY OF WELLINGTON

VICTORIA UNIVERSITY PRESS
Victoria University of Wellington
PO Box 600 Wellington
vup.victoria.ac.nz

ISBN 9781776561933

A catalogue record is available at the National Library of New Zealand

Published with the assistance of a grant from

ARTS COUNCIL OF NEW ZEALAND *TOI AOTEAROA*

Printed in China by 1010 International

Contents

Lawns

I am the least difficult of men. All I want is boundless love.
—Frank O'Hara

text message

up close and matesy   with warbler
this morning   letting me watch
no worries   not shy   warbling
followed by   thundering farm trucks
probably   filled with little lambs
                                              it's

the slaughtering   season

You Are Here

1

. . . introductions

What do you do when you move somewhere new?

You visit the graveyard first thing   to look   for immigrants
look for babies   look for old folks   look for siblings   look for
confirmed   bachelors   look   for newlyweds

Look for   unholy   deaths &   hermits
See if their graves are well tended   Look for those who vanished
into the bush   look   for the hint of a plague

Look for someone with your name   look   for someone
with your age   Look at the flowers & wonder
who it was   out of all the people at the supermarket

who put those flowers there   The week you moved here
one of the staff was   murdered in his flat
There is a memorial plaque   He shares   one quarter of your name

2

. . . domestic

In the homegrown graveyard   where
private grass   grows long

goldfinches   spool old cobwebs off
retired   lilac   faces   All the

statues   cracked & broken
left to   soften in the weather

have now softened
to the point   where they feel clucky

& provide
soft furnishings   for finches

3

. . . return

tomb   stones   ar   rive   in   south   er ly sets

Go   out to Tora   see the wrecks &   sweat
watching surfers fall around   all that daggery rust

Squint & say   it's big out there   to tōrea   who turn   who run
who laugh   they say   ha ha go home   ha ha go home go home

Saw a ripple on a hill that marked   a triumph or the fallen
Saw a seal   saw a big dead bird   move   softly at the edge

Next time you're at the graveyard   look for shipwreck epitaphs
Next time you're at the graveyard   look for epitaphs that say

died doing what he loved

& then
go home
go home

Kārearea

she turned her ear
said *falcon*   we left
our cups & rushed

outside to stand
with heads kicked back &
eyes cross checking sky

found faint manu tukutuku
translucent & ferocious
& delicate as a mote

When Birds Pronounce Their Short Metal Scrapes
& Withering Twirls

G says the third eye resides near Kaitoke

G has to go to the city   all those people   it does his head in   but

G can count on feeling   a lift   as he passes Kaitoke   he feels a
magnetic change   because of the third eye   the fact of it
residing near Kaitoke

G likes it here & he likes a yarn   He'll yarn about
governmental lizards & how tap water's good for washing one thing
that one thing being your brain

G grins   asks about the work   how's it coming   did that mortar
do the trick & he hopes I'm wearing a mask   I buy cement
& paint from G cos the   yarns & the   10% discount

From tall pines
shading   lumber   yard
young tūī   only knows   one song
Five rounded husky tolls like a   resonant microwave

People from the Pit Stand Up

1

. . . scene

In the park a boy   who leans on good brown thighs
says his father was an All Black   & an arsehole   so who are you

In the park a soldier   spins heroics then he dies
People   do live here & have full & active lives

Husbands   lean on mowers & consider their good fortune
Mopping grinny brows   They know when something's valuable

They cast back over shoulders   in mimes of calling wives
People do   live here & have full & active lives

Girl's got something going on but no one says a word

Dude's gotta go up north with his tail between his legs

Baby found a kitten   she wields it like a prize

People do live here & have full & active lives

2

. . . score

Everyone   fat & gothic at the train station this morning
A homicidal fog hums orange   good thing I didn't   oh haha

Magpies   cut a   curdled song like   days   before   Apple   when
people had to   whistle   to show you what they mean

Train   came we   murmur   towards its   breathy   melody
low eyed we   surge aboard   grey   obedient   Roman starlings

& at 7am the bells
go   *dingdingdingdingdingdingding*

Fog   soon falls away revealing stinging indigenous light &

. . . burning kahikatea stumps   up & down the valley

Passenger:
        did you see a man   shadowy   at the foot of the mountain?

Passenger:
        what   is a ten-letter word for the   end of the world?

Bellbird:
        now a dirge picked up   from a church outside of   Masterton

while kererū
        cascade like kids
                whose whole damn class has
                                been dismissed

3

. . . costume

People tuck their faces tight
a consequence of katabatic wind   no sea to catch it

People pull their chins right in
a consequence of brittle pride   eye contact can crush it

People laugh like tender bullies
a consequence of   this is it

& a real deep hurt cos   this is it

People fear new eloquences rolling off the hill
People value curtains drawn & a   smack around the ears will fix ya

We wear

gumboots
with our bathrobes
to the dairy
when it rains

oh

4

. . . cuisine

Shop veges
brushed into piles like

dust because
everyone has a garden so go home   plant zucchinis

Humidity
in the foothills results in a   bumper crop of zucchinis

People
knock on doors & ask if   anyone needs zucchinis

The chip shop
is in surplus chips what with everyone   eating zucchinis

Children
are getting creative re   the glut of zucchinis

Alas   there is no real nutritional gain   from eating so many

zucchinis

5

. . . romance

In the winter I planted flaxes
& they've taken
tall & muscular
now it's spring
so I sleep naked
& when that suckerpunch
wind comes down
it makes those hard shafts slap
slide like lovers legs in showers

Go step outside go feel it
go stand naked in the flaxes
to get one physical fix

It's   a wasteland

in the countryside &   devastation in the bedroom
I laugh . . .

but I'm hard-edged too
That's the bad result

6

. . . publicity

Hey
ya fake it till ya make it

There's a flash cheese shop in this town   So   between   getting
pissed & stealing shit try a   truffle oil brie

A famous journalist   described the town as a nest
of molesters & addicts   & the whole place sighed

over this undeniable historic truth   All the same
it's nice to be noticed   Does she know we have a

cheese shop now?   It's easy enough
in a crowded café   to think a man is speaking Portuguese

but this isn't the city   this   isn't the city
this   is not the city   this

is a loaded   frontier   with fromagerie

7

. . . bouquet

a pretty weed   something   something
a smooth twig to finish it off

for himself   not his lover
not his mother or his friend
the flowers are for himself
for when he gets home
for on the table
for when he opens the door
for it will be nice to see
for
for

for he is a disgrace
        a disgrace
        a disgrace
        a disgrace
        a disgrace
        a disgrace
        a disgrace   but

in 2003 when Debbie K   revealed   she buys flowers for herself
he stored this fact like   batteries baked beans pack of cigs
bottled water flashlight whisky   All it takes   sometimes   is a posy

8

. . . coda

re the assorted defences   displayed in our yards like bowers
re the flapping stickmen of eager children we   wear in our eyes

re lovers   like the dollars   brief   re kindnesses   inflicted
re meannesses   a slimmer fit   *my regards to the people*

re staple dives   re middle class pies   re pig dogs   pigs &   olives
re all the pearls   that sag around   *my regards   to the people*

&

re the local boy   who hovers on sprinter's thighs   && says
his father went around the world   & one day so will he

& muthafuckas best watch out

like   *best of luck*

& a toast   to the people

Sensitive Boys

Sooty shearwater   glancing off ripples

Like Lisa at Lisa's Hairdressers   inspecting dampened curls

Like browsing at the fabric store   when there's nothing
that needs sewing   but everything needs touching

Sooty shearwater   smallest petrel   Why are petrels called petrels?
Petrels   are called petrels after St Peter who walked on water

I guess he was a dancer too   & probably rather dainty   Old Peter
What was his story?

        Peter was a fisherman & number one disciple
        Peter was the first Pope & emotionally unstable

        I can't find anything about dancing

Once I saw a fisherman reel his line in at Queens Wharf & unhook
a sooty shearwater who'd been pierced through the chest

. . . sooty shearwater   colour of   soot

Like a pianist at a piano after some time   away from the piano

first he strokes the keys   with the backs of his hands

Ballade

The mad poet says it's better than sex   throwing back her laugh
flashing teeth for a   startled   cameraman

I took her advice & I played it   after a rancid kiss   Made a crash
& a crash & who cares   if your octaves are ninths or sevenths
Afterwards   your hands should shake & maybe

                                                           . . . do you recognise
euphoric pill of the   recently hit   a tingling soda   red lung joy
             Last time I got smacked in the face I burst out laughing
the truly thankful hoot of baptist or of masochist . . .   people
who get into fights or fits cos they have to   *feel* something
Between spitting on mirrors & pouring the tea   we all want to
feel *something*   If there's no one around to bloody your nose
suck your dick & you're   bored of masturbation . . .
consider the piano   that mania enabler   Turn
to Ballade No. 1 &   rain down calamitous tolls:

    all   the buildings are falling
    all   the volcanoes are erupting
    all   the animals are in the kitchen   & the children

well   forget it

Suburban Rescue

This woman at the shops she said

is it you who plays the loud music?
& I said   uh oh   haha   is that good or bad!
& she said   I just want to tell you that I feel like I know you
& she had this awful husband

She said   I was so tired   It was me & the kids & I was   so tired
Fell asleep in a pile of laundry   about two in the afternoon & the girl
from next door   she saw me through the window   She came over
She sent me to bed   cleaned the house
Laundry   dishes   whole thing

& I said   once when I was very sad
my mother   came over with her powerful vacuum &
took care of the floors

We were both quiet for a moment   Then I said   any requests?
& she said
        I like it best   when Maria Callas   sets the hedge aquiver

On Isolation

Like   music practice under the cherry tree   I can think of
idyllic moments   Stripped down to shorts for rays   took a seat &
went over scores   After Bach a soft applause   I turned & saw
past washing-lines a man with name tag   clipboard   tight shine
hair & professional grin   Got up to meet him   semi naked &
embarrassed but hospitable   with a plan to say no thank you   turn
him away get back to etudes   But Rakesh got in quickly   said
though he'd come to talk providers   he had paused to listen first
Charmed   I said I'll hear your pitch & pulled a shirt from the line
We took our seats in dappled shade & Rakesh outlined exciting
savings offered by his firm   First I thought his hair was black   but
as sun became an evening sun & solarised the flyaways I saw it was
the dark of brown that's cousin to magenta   Rakesh projected
savings of up to forty bucks a month   first bill on the house
Rakesh explained the small print & laughed at the company jargon
Rakesh shook his head in disbelief when I told him my current rates
Rakesh reiterated the savings at stake & then moved on to sport
the weather   music   travel   books & films   After signing up
(what else? what else?) Rakesh asked for a tune   Just before I go
he said   I'd love it please play something   Now a little bit
in love   I said Rakesh ok   & played him the Arensky theme &
Rakesh closed his eyes

Next we were supposed to kiss & have sex   right there in the
garden   But Rakesh was probably just a nice dude & not into
dudes per se   Well I've got his number   Maybe one day I'll have a
reason to call like   Rakesh   there is a gas leak
Then ask when he shows up   Rakesh   what colour is your hair

Speaking Diary

Tuesday
hey buddy (to a dog)

Wednesday
thanks (to Diane at checkout)

Friday
put on my robe and slipped
pre-coffee onto the porch   whispered
she changed her name to Deveraux
to the logging trucks of dawn

Saturday
thanks (to Diane at checkout)

Monday
lay in the bath   listened
to the fridge   purr and clear
its throat   for a moment
I thought it just might say
Sam   how was your day?

Tuesday
thanks (to Diane at checkout)

Blood Work

1

. . . prologue

looked around the house today
at all my sharp-nosed
husbands

there are thirty bags of mud
should I require another
husband

2

. . . instructions

Make a man
to help with labour

Make a man
to protect your neighbour

Make a man
to prove your mystical depth

Make a man
to show off your technical breadth

Make a man
because you're new here but a golem will be newer

Make a golem
because safety in numbers

To make a man
make the shape of a man then use
god's name to
bring him life

To make a man
count your kilos & then phone Wendy to order the difference

To make a man
use Buff Raku Trachyte

Buff Raku Trachyte
achieves a lovely oatmeal buff   Firing to reduction achieves a
gorgeous satin brown with   beady katipō speckle
That's the   trachyte coming through

Buff Raku Trachyte
is a forgiving & open-minded clay   ideal
for handbuilding & slab-work   It says as much on the label
& you can be sure that it's the truth   Everyone agrees
down at the WPA   & Wendy is terrific
Fast delivery & a discount   when you buy in bulk

To make a man
shape him out of clay
then walk or dance around him
saying letters from the alphabet
& the secret name of god

To make a man
consider your kit   Large batt   scraped clean   not warped
Banding wheel   the low rise kind   wide   it's a tremendous help
Old toothbrush   container for water   Add a splash of vinegar for a
more effective binder   Modelling tools   You can spend a few bucks
getting these in town   But I find a four-mil crochet hook turns
all the marks I need   That & a book-length lightweight knife   non-
serrated with comfortable grip   If you don't have these things already
pop along to your local op shop   Ask Wendy
to add the banding wheel to your   Buff Raku Trachyte order

To make a man
prepare the body
then write on his forehead
aleph mem tav
spelling out
TRUTH
this will bring him to
LIFE
erase the aleph to spell
DEATH

When making a man
consider your health   Mind the broom   don't sweep
You'll agitate all that dust   & clay dust is full of silica which'll
settle in your lungs & leave you with silicosis   Then you're dealing
with the same sorts of medical bills as a lifelong smoker   so
don't sweep   Use a vacuum   Mop daily   Wear a mask if it gives you
peace of mind   I tend to just hold my breath

To make a man
prepare the body then write
god's name
onto parchment put the
parchment into his mouth

To make a man
begin with the feet   Wield a slab of clay the size of a short piece of
two-by-four   Hold it like the butcher with his fresh young cut
firmly in two hands   Chin up   chest out   stand sure
on the ground where you will not sweep   Hold
your Buff Raku Trachyte flesh   Feel   the weight of its rage
Slam it onto your batt   step back

To make a man
consider your neighbour   You may build with best intentions & still
find blood on your hands   So stash your hammer & carry a knife

If your man does *run amok*
If he *threatens innocent lives*

the creator should remove
the Divine Name
rendering him
incomplete
or unfinished
like an embryo

To kill a man
remove the parchment

To kill a man
erase the aleph

To kill a man
work in reverse

But first
throw colour at his body

For sex
For wealth
For history
For art
For class
For empathy

& turn him towards the wall
Go to sleep with locks on the doors
If by morning   nobody's heart has softened

Take a hammer to his temple

3

. . . some considerations

All this
gives me a bad bad back &
probably emphysema &
concerns   like for example

this old knife is broken

&

is obsession a problem

Blue is an aspiration
Pink is lazy   black is hard   &
gold   gold   Gold is on my mind

Look into the face of the boy
see what he has to say

        He might ask for a   quick death   or

                to be held by the shoulders & kissed

4

. . . life model

He's ugly   He's a sex bomb   If you told him he was *beautiful*
he'd tell you that he's *ugly*   He'd agree that he's a *sex bomb*
but beautiful makes him *yawn*   When we're together I consider his
uneven nose   Consider his nostrils built to flare   Consider his teeth
Uneven also   Observe that one of them is grey   He's always
smaller than I remember   I'm a yak thug when I'm with him
Could carry him partway up a mountain   He has a new scar on his
brow & a pimple on his cheek   His hair still loves the pillow
He smells like a 3pm lunchbox   But under his clothes he ripples
cut as a surfer with a loose jar of olives   & his bag is filled
with books   but books on India & transcendence & dead
philosophers talking bullshit about time spent with famous poets
Twice a week he drops his shorts & models for a class   They draw
him as Atlas & embryo   They draw him ugly as knotted trees &
magnificent like a horse   Sometimes
I get a bit hot   Preparing inanimate arms & legs
I have to   take a deep turn round the bedroom before getting back
       & he's ugly   He's a sex bomb   a cowboy nympho
in his own words   He's smart   He's got that bag of books
Plays piano in nine-eight   He visits   Strikes the archer's pose
& I see he is clay flesh made manifest   That he is all clay men &
beautiful   When he laid down his hand-turned limbs   I saw
that if he stuck around I might one day have to kill him   I said

you'd better hurry up & explode

cowboy   & then get the hell outta of my house

42

5

. . . further to your health

If you're sculpting in the summer & Cheryl texts for a g&t   don't
say yes just because she's your pal   The building process is
time-sensitive   Unscheduled breaks can fuck shit up
Tell her you'll see how things go & then forget to text her back
Apologise in the morning & make vague promises about next week
It's normal to become seriously involved   with a man you're
building from scratch   Time becomes singly focussed
As with all affairs   some friends might raise a brow

6

. . . make your own damn truth

Where were all the boys
when I was pretty & nineteen?

They were in my head &
I didn't have cocktail money

Dude wants flowers for his visions
Tryin' on all kinds of lies

Dude wants juice from persimmon
To trickle on his thigh

Where were all the boys   I had them
in my head   got paid

now this house of cocks is chockablock
Fifty faces to a room

they guard their lie they
lie in wait

For me to get out my carving knife
& inscribe the name of god

7

. . . newborn

Body wrapped in a blue tarpaulin

not ready for the elements but

this rain came to test   vitreosity &

this wind came to test his footing so I

got him all wrapped

he's a big boy too

two metres tall & all

wrapped up in blue

a thin white rope

to keep him bundled like

meat

(a comparison he'd be thrilled by)

my ceramic Scarecrow   organ

aspirational   he's my

clay Tin Man

8

. . . muscles

because none of us are athletes
we play piano
we play jokes

we run till knees give out
we run till ankles break
these people are in their thirties

but who needs sport anyway
in order to compete
go stand in a room full of artists

bet the round
when nerves will be shattered
& it's physical   too

to wield the tools
to make an eight-foot man
to make him look like he'd sweat

9

. . . constructed skin

Mine is the only hairy chest
These babies have no follicles
Their pores are sealed with lumbersider
Clearasil Ultra wouldn't help
Rogaine Xtra wouldn't help

Mine is the only hairy chest

If that makes me the silverback
fine I'll be the silverback
I'll pick my feet & snore
around the terracotta harem

I touch & I touch & I am never touched

These babies   determined &   peering
through the owl light   believing
themselves into existence

Which is easier to do in the gloom & I wonder
          if I touched them now
                    might I feel a little heat

10

. . . clay man speaks

& HE SAYS
Mostly I stand around & fade
I wasn't made to be held
I find a mark   I meditate
The furniture   the piano
Everything gets dusty   my complaints aren't unique
I'm glad the piano gets regular   action   my mate
Keeping his smile bright   offering up a tune
Even when his pate & throat are muffled in thin velveteen

Tell me   why did you make a man?

> *– I made a man because at least two people in my life*
> *have suggested intimacy is important*

& HE SAYS
Well I'm here   when you arrive
I'm here   in the lounge   the garage   the hall
Panhandlers for the general   aesthetic   you and me
See the hooligan line I cut against your eggshell wall?

> *– Yeah   yeah I do*

& HE SAYS
But still you're prowling for intimacy?
I hear you've lost your mojo

— I go out walking & it's ping ping ping! *Then I turn into*
the driveway & it's like I've had   all my lobotomies at once

Hey what's it like to be a man?   I remember
pressing my fingers all around your muddy conception

& HE SAYS
The memory is fossilised in my skin
Put your face to my face and describe it

— Oh!   you're so cold

& HE SAYS
I'm indoors   south-facing   the sun only proven
by your   faint   colouring   when you pass in February   Tell me
what's it like to make a man?

—   It's like being a jaded plastic surgeon   shopping
for expensive shoes   I feel bored then   reckless
then successful then   bored then   embarrassed
I practise a sort of   projected scarification
Tell me   did you ever feel triumphant?
What's it like   to be a man?

& HE SAYS
Like a retired rent-boy   ill-adjusted
still eager to please   My friends
are dead or have moved away
Mostly I eavesdrop on pianos
I just stand around & fade

11

. . . it's good to live in a house full of golems

Last night I gave a studio tour   but in a private mood
Held the hand of a clay man like   my first day of school

It's good to live in a house full of golems   In the summer
when my bike was nicked   me asleep down the hall   hot night
all the doors flung open   I hope those thieves poked their noses in
& lit up the room with their phones   eyes peeled for iPads & laptops
        illuminating instead the terrible faces of nudes who loom
I'll bet if those thieves poked their noses in   they scrammed
pretty quick after that   I'll bet they said what the fuck is this
           took my piece a shit bike & scrammed

It's good to live in a house full of golems   When people
come around   I don't have to perform solo   I can say

here is a man in pink   I can say here is a man in gold
I can say here is a man who drank neon through a straw   till he was
three-quarters neon runway   & one-quarter family album
I can say here is a man who falls for   charismatic drunks
I can say hope it's a real good time   Any questions I'm in my lair

12

. . . installation day

The man with the hi-ab says make it nice & tight like a German girl
He laughs & says you liked that one   He says whaddidya missus say?
when I shake out the sheets to wrap things up   He says
yer old lady still in bed when you ripped those sheets right off 'er?
He says to ask the bloke from the shop or else you'll get that black
cunt   When P crouches down to help he says never trust a woman
He says all this of an afternoon   installing sculptures in a vineyard

The man with the hi-ab is good   he's good   he's a brute he does a
good job   I'd like to stop asking him but I'm wary   of bad blood
In the main it's brutes you get   hiring hi-abs in the sticks
I say this as if the city is free of misogyny & bigots   The city's just
better at lying   Maybe it's good that this bleary old creep waxes
camply about bitches & fags   At least you know to avoid him
Ah well   he's Bernsteinian at the hydraulics   Paganinian
with a welding flame

& P stood her ground   said   mate   mate
                                   I grew up with shearing gangs
                                   so do your worst

                                                      & she snapped off a rose

51

13

. . . installed

See them stare across damp farms

towards surf & whipped-up action

We're forty minutes from the coast

so they look with their longest eye   It's a triumph

                                                to build men who dream of

                                                paddling out at dawn

14

. . . you're gonna be a star

From under Karamean mountains

From sunken Northland stadiums

From Australia's powdered metal rim

Wrapped & stamped in a Chinese industrial zone

& sent south to the Wairarapa

to prepare for a number up north again

up in Auckland probably

He bears no ill will   just indifference

He bears no resemblance either

to his gravelly whakapapa

His desires now are glittery

People drink expensively

at his elbow

They don't

dig

15

. . . spin

Call that gold a self-portrait
& people will believe it

even
if it's never been the truth!

no truer than my piano skills   no truer than my bedroom skills
no truer than my dancing skills   it depends on who else is present

no truer than my childhood   such sparkling mythology
no truer than my twenties   that decade

of weird fitting   Now go to the gallery
                                                see all of my noses

                                                        so Roman
                                              this Jew could be minted

                                          a small buffed nickel portrait
                                                   with one value that's

                                                          for sure

16

. . . press

'13

Using the vessel as a starting point   I cross-checked similar types of work (i.e. wood-fired ashy bowls against ashy bowls, arrangements of tall slender vessels)   I make ware that is recognisable as the classical pottery vessel   A pod is a capsule or vessel   *Stickin' Around* is a wheel-thrown vessel   These vessels hint at being filled with something thick and unctuous   In gathering up these sand-blasted pieces and re-firing them with new clay into the united form of a new vessel I attempt

'14

By amassing them together into a vessel form I attempt   robust, sculptural, functional vessels   In my work there exists the juxtaposition of tradition against the sculptural vessel along with the evolution of   Vessels   Vessels   Three woman [sic]   Vessels My ceramic practice continues to use the vessel as a means of exploring   the form transitions into a softer more tactile vessel   I liken the vessel to feelings of containment

'15

I have sought to address the traditional views of the vessel and containment   The flame created its own path through the stack and deposited salt vapour near the vessel   The work is a ceramic pinhole camera that is based on the domestic vessel   I have chosen to make the work resemble a domestic vessel   [I] create delicate vessels

17

. . . salon des refusés

Amber panes keep them lit like drunks
broke in a motey bar
former dandies in the gloom
Their heads nod towards the puckered glass
yellow flowers
in condemned grass

Tallest with his pointy chin
paraded once in Wellington
(& a grim half day in Masterton)
now he wears a crocheted wrap
whole face one cataract of dust
He knows Chopin by heart

Smallest in his flower vest
this chap's the one true portrait
So true that no one wanted him
creeping around their foyer

Pool boy with the bitchy hip was blue
for a city photoshoot
then burned a mean décolletage
for a seaside college bash
Now he stands to gloat but mate you failed   you failed

Still he wears that gaudy rose
pinned like a winner's sash

18

. . . requiem

In my dirty corner paddock
        an hour south of Eketāhuna

trucks pass by
        logs & livestock

half a truck-length from this pillow
        its head-shaped jewel

Trucks rumble through the scrim
        to deliver seismic dreams

& when the hills do stretch   well I have
        gristle & hips to sway with

Those dirt boys
        in the workroom though

locked knees & rigid ankles
        lousy surfers

they tripped & fell
        bird-bone fingers all over the floor

Afterwards on the phone
        much concern regarding the boys

are they ok the boys?
        the boys?

Oh I lost a boy
        look he's all over the floor

found a finger in the garden
        a penis in the grass

sure must have been a violent shake
        to get thrown way out there

No more trucks the next few days
        while slips are cleared from the hill

& I went out
        felt the earth move with a

dude from the shearing gang
        sheep huddled by electric fence

& farmers
        in their tractors pass

wide-eyed &
        disappointed

19

. . . befriend the blurry silhouette

Dreamed I found a clay man   nude & malleable in my bed   Lay
fleshily   against his rough brown belly & pushed   all the way in
Took his ear   in my   mouth &   felt it   dissolve

He said   *I love you Sam I love you*   & I   gripped his clammy arse
till it burst through my fingers like   soap   I pumped him till he
wilted   a loose exhausted hide & then I pumped the crumpled hide

He said   *I love you Sam I love you*   & he tasted good or   like
sand   & I pumped
& I pumped & I pumped & I pumped & I   pumped the muddy pile

So ok
here is a   sex life via
rough   objectophiliac   sleep flickerings

When the only faces
in all the days are those   one's manifested
one can expect   seepage

I've never
hashtagged IRL
why make such a distinction

20

. . . sometimes you look in the mirror & ask

how many clay men does one man need?   Probably not many   &
maybe I'd like a man who can sing   crack an egg   rub sore bones
I've practised enough with these   mannequins   I'm done making
rigid-wristed placeholder golems   This wand wants to
tap something new   like   For my next act
I'll tag kitchens with   found bucket lists   For my next act
I'll write a libretto   for papier mâché drag queens   to perform
under falling leaves   For my next act I'll   fall in love
If you ever see me start a new clay man   say
HEY!   BACK OFF!   STEP AWAY!
Then put me on a plane to Barcelona

                                                        People quit
They change their minds   One polyurethaned prime minister
remember   quit with zero notice   Just racked off to play
golf in Hawai'i   Yet half the population still revere him as messianic

My last clay man will have a   frying-pan arse & beer gut &
a withering chin & his skin   will be a   bloodless whorl of
daguerreotype damaged   wet newspaper
blown into corner   sun-stiffened   removed with spatula
propped up & considered   in Auckland from November
After that   who knows

Auckland (epilogue)

Jeff was there
he came on over
Everyone shook hands
Everyone said gidday Jeff
& Jeff said gidday
& gidday Graeme what's news from Christchurch
& Graeme said yep yep yep
& Jeff said speakin' of Christchurch

I had this public piece down there   When the time came to finally
deinstall I   put out cones   got my sledgehammer out & this old
bloke comes by   grabs the sledgehammer   says   good I hate
this fucken piece a shit   but he was old & he couldn't lift the thing
& he didn't know I was the artist   he thought I was just some other
poor bloke who didn't like the sculpture either   that I'd come on
down to wreck it

Everyone threw back their heads & roared
or else they put their hands on their knees
& leaned towards Jeff eyes delightedly
popped & incredulous   But that's art
said Jeff   they don't always approve
& we all said oh yeah
can't please everyone
I mean   shit
Time for tea

Nudes on Loan

1
. . . sightseeings

Ha last time I was in Auckland
this end of downtown
searching for a park & busting for a pee
I pulled up squirming to the Hilton
minimum parking fee twenty-five bucks
took pause cos twenty-five bucks
but I had to pee so bad I just rammed the car diagonal

       Plus I was late for the ferry to Tiri
       though when I got to the jetty they told me
              no ferries to Tiri till Wednesday
    Well shit I'd paid that twenty-five bucks
    I'd had plans to be a tourist . . .

Kōkako sunset deferred
I headed on uptown   to view the northern boys

Viewed   Jamaican dude
with killer thighs who lived in a flash apartment
Viewed   Chinese dude
with killer abs who lived in a shithole garage

Then went back to   Albany
to watch *Blind Date* with N
She was like
twenty-five bucks!

2

. . . full-length mirror

everyone's   putting out in public &   werkin' best reflections

clocked   in walk-in-wardrobes loos shop windows hubcaps &
backs of phones   we twirl   we   tuck pout pucker   highlight
we hide   we   reveal

like

birds of paradise   famously &   ba   boons   well   &
the dog   with her pheromones   mongrels at the gate   &

those who ask for   photographic   proof of   bandied talent

if the hour is right   you might get a
sequinned wink from the moon   boys

it's when the light is low that
hairy pots start to look real nice

3

. . . shopping

largest   flower   reeks   of   meat &
what's   more honest than   degradation

I'm here
Door is open
ok

we're liberated   teched-up   playboy   beasts in   lust &
low   electric

in a
windowless room on Queen St
with a kid who keeps asking
you ok you ok & you tell him
YES I'm ok I'm ok I'm ok
& you   spin him around

Morning   dressed & eloquent   stroll
into public galleries   go check out the   nudes on loan

4

. . . Paul Rosano Reclining

Who is Paul Rosano?   He's a long-limbed low-hum swarthy man
with loose wave afro & Disney Prince eyes & he's comfortable
with his body   He likes it   naked   on red couches   looking up
at you   at Sylvia   I think she likes him more than   he likes her &
I think he likes himself more than anyone   he has that
smug look of the invited   Hey he's handsome
like John Stamos if John Stamos was from Spain & let his hair grow
long &   didn't shave for a week & was   fractionally more angular
Was Paul Rosano on TV?   Have I seen a mandolin?
The way he lies with one knee cocked & his cock curled like a warm
pet   & his arm thrown up into scalloped coiff   & his pit hair
fanned like a cockatoo's crest   I could lower a lute
right over him &   some tune would emerge   honeyed & invisible
as from theremins   Paul Rosano   sexy stranger from a
wet   suburban   dream   His odour fills the gallery like
he's not had time to bathe   between lovers   Lazy
sonofabitch   Still I'm crushing   on Paul Rosano

5

. . . everything is going to be ok

                              I'm not the only bumpkin with
Beyoncé in his heart   btw   who sheds his swannie & paints his
lips to glisten in the city   Holla   if you recognise the
small sashaying animal that   grows like a starry-eyed tumour in one's
zipped-up rural armpit   & you visit metropolitan slopes
to let it run around unzipped   & it's sweaty & charming   & lit
like a boozy   dungeon   musical but   you're careful to leave
before it turns into the   Kronos Quartet-scored reboot
which is tough cos the talent's so perfectly formed   &
saying no is   well   you don't   you just say   yes yes
till   every   thing   gets   quiet

    On the plane home   I sat behind a man who was
    reading poems   & I was also reading poems!
    I hoped the flight attendant would notice &   say out loud
    something like   hey

        two people reading poems

   so that other people might hear & say

                My heart's aflutter!

                       etc.

text message

how is the afterglow?

text message

see you tomorrow
sun-kissed   kissed
generally   &
quite happy in the end

saw two dotterels at
Whatipu

don't want to get
married anyway

Further Studies

Amedeo Modigliani

Teenagers dig long necks   Check out any portfolio circa 1998
Amedeo was a Jew who liked cocaine & sex & I imagined a
brotherhood between us   more aspirational than anything real
Anyway   by the time I was twenty there were   too many women

Edward Gorey

Most moody queers have clocked him   Edward was a ballet fan &
mate of Frank O'Hara   I felt an affinity & imagined a
brotherhood between us   Pages of dandies in mascara   If they
weren't in their bathing suits they were   swaddled in fur or velvet
Whether wealthy or poor everybody wore the same dainty tennis
shoes   The pages sag with innuendo but I never found one kiss
People drown or are hit by lorries   & even then they remain
composed   I began to get blue balls

Francis Upritchard

Francis was born in New Plymouth   built a world & took it
to the Venice Biennale   men made from bakeable polymer
I felt a procedural affirmation & a sisterhood in the modelling scene
In 2006 I had my first show   men made from bakeable polymer
Some of them fell to pieces   I was ashamed   Francis's men fall to
pieces too   but she isn't ashamed   Check out her patched skins of
graft & infill   Her people stoop in chequered cloaks & offer up
peeling grins   Lame penises sit ragged & temporary as wool
snagged on wire   Somebody ought to pick them up

Ramesh Nithiyendrin

His penises are permanent   His dicks go all the way down & weigh
as much as a leg   Ramesh is six years younger than me & wins all
the Australian prizes   He makes stacked ceramic self-portraits that
strut messily gold-toothed grins   They slide inside red blue black skin
that drips around jewellery & pools in crooks   He signs his name
like this   RAMS   in fast spraypaint on plinths   He possesses a
loose drapery that I admire & fear & covet   & I feel a kinship
naturally   cos of the clay cock scene   so I follow him on Instagram
But I reckon he might like my poem more than my pricks   which are
timid   Anyway shout out to you Ramesh   I mentioned your name
to RW at the pub & he said I should stop being a pussy   To take
note & make erections that   explode into marble foyers   Okay

Fred

Fred has painted ten black lines   pawed   smears
going all the way down   He's two years old & Recognised
A hero   in the neighbourhood scene   Picasso
said it most famously   So when did I first fear the crayon?
I want an affinity with Fred   This is my aspiration

Notes for a Dinner Party

What is your inspiration?
mens' 10 high heels   salted ground   lame peacocks   harrier towns

What is your inspiration?
to lie with beautiful men & to lie
to talented men   & to lie
around rough-cast men & to lie
because   pure truths became   pollen clouds a long time ago

What is your inspiration?
probably some kind of pollen cloud from   a long time ago

What is your inspiration?
I drink my soup   I sit with the feeling

. . . low white sun   . . . wicked pine   . . . damp crater
where you find good rocks & put them   in your pocket   *what*
is your inspiration oh my God I'm telling you!   December

I went to Australia to discover a
new box of colour but all I got
was a sopping T-shirt &
somebody else's
stupid
sun   goodnight

Kim Hill Interviews a Famous Artist

Kim Hill is flabbergasted and spits into the mic
Are you talking metaphorically or actually because _____ you're an artist
The artist doesn't tell lies
The artist says his art and his belief system are one and the same

Are you talking metaphorically or actually because _____ you're an artist
The artist asks   do you find it demanding?
The artist says his art and his belief system are one and the same
Kim Hill suggests he said that so she can express incredulity

The artist asks   do you find it demanding?
The artist says no one needs an education to look at art
Kim Hill suggests he said that so she can express incredulity
The artist says everyone has a vote and the mistakes   he throws them away

The artist says no one needs an education to look at art
Kim Hill says there are people listening and crying out no no no
The artist says everyone has a vote   the mistakes   he throws away
Kim Hill recovers herself and asks a question about Buddhism

There are people listening and crying out   no no no
The artist says there's a type of Buddhism where you can drink and have sex
Kim Hill recovers herself and asks a question about Saturn Cycles
The artist suggests that marriage is about freedom

The artist found a version of Buddhism where you can drink and have sex
        The time is   nine fifty-nine and   pips   are   imminent
The artist suggests that marriage is about freedom
Kim Hill is flabbergasted and spits into the mic

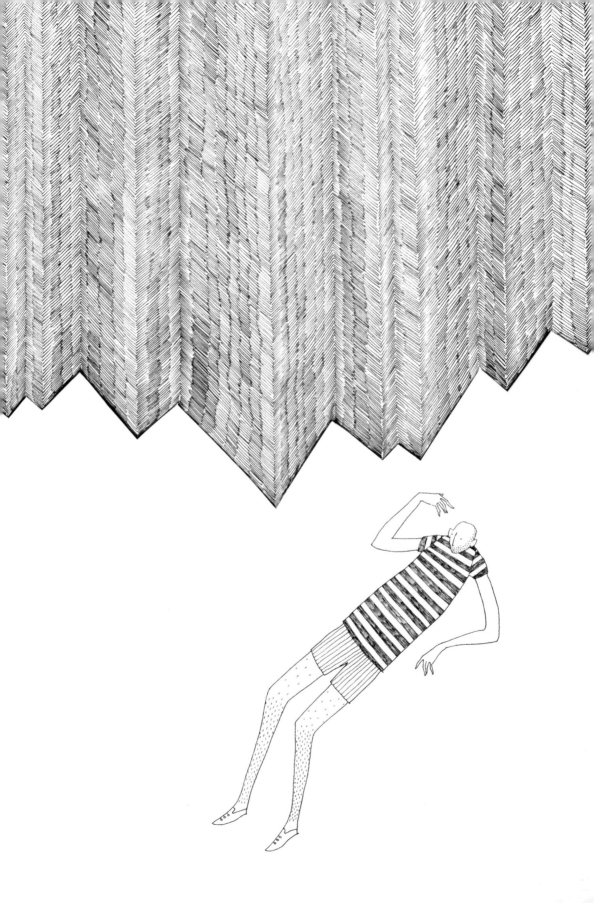

One Good Way to Stay Big in an Empty House

The liar in his lidded room   filled with mutes & static   needs to
protect himself   from truths that wink when the sun goes down

He could take a long pull   cast down the bottle   stalk halls with a
wax ballast bobble head   He could wear long scarves draped loose
so they whip around like   fawning staff

He could leave the dishes undone   the illusion of recent parties
He could keep a tidy kitchen   the illusion of imminent guests

He could settle in with the   geniuses maestros prodigies & darlings
who camp all over his bookshelves   Revisit maybe
Drawing from life &   visions &   everyday visions & induced visions
& dreams that took place right here in this house which is   empty
& he's   just an   edge-of-the-village fantasist   with a
hook-up to bookshop prescriptions

He could draw a face in a journal   for one kind of conversation
He could add a cock & balls to it   for one kind of flirtation

He could carve a thigh   cut a neck from clay   for one obvious kind
of foreplay   See his stacked up tools for limbular builds
It's a   sand-stormed veterans hospital . . .   & he makes
all manner of erections

The liar takes a boozy nap   puts pillow in a limp embrace

Tomorrow   he'll buy another book   Antarctica or   Nudes

Two Ways of Going to Sleep

Think about the seaweed
      & how nobody works harder than seaweed
Seaweed tosses out its hair   gathers it up in a towel   tosses it out again
      Seaweed practises lunges for all tomorrow's marathons
Seaweed has Bob Marley   on   repeat
      skanking till a southern bully changes the track to metal
Watching seaweed is like chanting *om*
      Watching seaweed I throw up my hands & say   oh   my   god
Watching seaweed gives me an anxious gut & the beginnings of a twitch
      Watching seaweed I miss my mum's soft hip to burrow into & be still
Watching seaweed wears me out
      Or rocks
Rocks wear me out   up a river with rapids
      Cool hands clearing faces with maniacal chuckle
Their entire lives are one long exfoliation treatment
      Beauty therapy for fatalist monks who accept a sandy repurposing
Rocks most weary at the coast
      Waterboarded by sadist waves who seek no truth or confession
Rocks take lifelong guttural gasps like they've fluid on the lungs
      Rocks stroked like dolls in lunatic asylums till every single one is bald
Rocks wear me out
      Every eyelash fished from my eye is promptly followed by another
Hey baby go to sleep
      you have the privilege of sentience
                 & animation
                   now   be
                        shhhhhhhhhhh

How Female-Admirer Dream Narratives Run Rampant Through the Gay Collective Unconsciousness: Two Reports

1

yellow cliffs above the bay   where a boy lives in a lean-to &
a waterfall runs through it   I wave proposals from dinghies
The boy at his elevation   can see   ripples   peal out
adrenalin-hued   from my small tin boat   I hide
I hide in dinghies from C   who thinks we are lovers after I
kissed her   on the lips   by accident   Then after she found the
note I sent   to the boy   she   unravelled   all of my
crochet scarves   & hats   in a rage

2

He met a girl at a party   Her name was Antigone   She was smooth
& round & blond & she blushed with thin eyes & an in-on-it grin
She flopped down onto the bed & said   let's get married   He said
you're great Antigone   but let me get back to you on that   Then he
lost his phone & all his numbers & figured that's that re Antigone
But the following week she wandered into his room   she said   hi
remember me   & they fell playfully onto the bed   & Antigone
propped herself on an elbow & said   I do love you but I'm a lesbian
plus I've never been kissed   He said Antigone that's terrific   I'm
gay so that's terrific   btw   you're so beautiful & hilarious to boot
so how have you never been kissed?   & Antigone sighed & dropped
dramatically onto the sheets again   A boy came
to the front door then   left the papers on the porch
& a warm wind blew   carried the papers away
        let them fall all over the yard

Lawns

1

. . . unmown

He cares

neglect is *ok*
because

lawn care is to die by gradual fade
& long grass is an adequate understudy

for the sea when there is
no sea

2

. . . slippery slope

Then nor'westerlies come on down
     to chop green wavelets so they slap
          sides of houses leaving   long blades
               stuck to weatherboards   wind-whipped
                   snot   on a child's cheek

Akimbo at the window
     considering the horizon
          supposed to   clear up this afternoon
             will get the   mower   out then

Sad dad
     Swimming pool
          P T A
             Picket fence
                Chocolate box misery
                    Icon

Goodbye youth
     dreams   *hey!*
          Just get on & do it mate   it's
          not the end of the world
          & the neighbourhood
          will approve

3

. . . mown

It all gleams false & permanent
washed   newly laid

He cares!
& the neighbourhood approves

of all this rindless pounamu
setting under English boughs

The dandelions
are dead now   so

he lingers   with new observations

      notes   . . . we could do with a little rain

Such commentary   now stock in trade
as the heat of rebellion   fades

4

. . . of the poets

JD does his once a week
JB has plans for mangling

MD is reminded of lawns when out
shopping for kimonos

KC can't start her mower
At the party last night somebody said

& leaves of grass by you know you know
till W said WW & we all got drunk & read aloud

felt bourgie & I liked it
Well so oh cool I'm a poet then

I've written about lawns
grass

about lawn care
& how I avoid it

Just let the grass grow long
& lie down in it

. . . apart from moths & love & loss
lawns seem to be the thing

for serious poets
defined

by the states & traits
of their lawn

MR bought a bench & set it
up in her raggy meadow

She likes it long & I like her
We hear the same suburban death march

veiled as upkeep
We don't mind how long blades stick

like snot to weatherboarded cheeks
HB won't mow her thistles

GO knows of a lawn that forgets
HM has no prickles

Something about high tides & disguises oh cool
I'm a serious poet

I can look out the kitchen window & see
that the grass is singing

famously
just like Doris said

5

. . . kibbutz 2001

For a while

I worked factory shifts   four till noon at the conveyor belt

Co-workers from Kiev & Beersheba   spoke gutturally
of looming invasions

I laughed   when the planes crashed into the towers
cos I didn't understand

but Oren grew fluent in English   long enough to tell me
you're a fool

That evening in the pub   we talked about annihilation
& in the morning I was transferred   to gardening detail   so

6

. . . gardening detail

I met a man with a   volleyball tan

I met a man with a   loose linen sleeve

he hung his shirts to dry   between the olive trees

In a hot place   I met a man   whose father was put on a train

I met a man   who dipped his head & swayed to summon the rain

In a desert   I met a man who knew   the way to an oasis

In a desert   twenty white camels moved their caravan around us

In a desert   I worked with a man who dug &   waited for a sign

& twenty white camels   materialised
              & an owl   quiet as curtains
           & a scorpion   muscled in the dunes

I knew a man whose gospel was   *make the desert bloom*

Here's a man   who on Monday   flew into a rage

& all the animals of the desert   fade   white

red   green   black   as the sun goes down

7

. . . reverie

Working up to weeding when the jails opened up & let out all their
arborists   Big men came like giraffes with brutalist philosophies
In cathartic rage they truncated tōtara to whiskers   Tossed trunks
like cabers into the harbour   Found ponga then uprooted them
Sent like javelins into the harbour   All those logs put out to sea
No slow weeding with the cricket on while these   criminals
are at work

Swam out towards the timber   Took long breaths & took
long strokes   Reached a buoyant branch to hug & practise
my main points   Clung like blooded flotsam till I
saw the fast man coming   He approached like a whale so I knew
he was boss   Scooped me up onto a prison barge where
buzzcut beefcakes lay   The boss's eyes were of atolls & his muscles
were of the sand   He kissed my neck & turned me around &
fucked me against the wall   Later
I watched him   pound a   figure skater from TV

8

. . . meanwhile   west of Kaiwaewae

When frosts float saggy from the south
moving through the local sty   sending piggy mist to settle

& one bird says   hey-you
& one bird says   be-jew-el
& one bird speaks for us all & says   wow-okay wow-okay wow-okay

you sort of shoulder yourself sideways   into lace-draped paddocks
All those tiny mirrors   just making the air more grass to cut

Cherry trees shed yellow leaves   shoals of koi in unwashed tanks
They've swarmed the town since '43   old site of POW camp

& one bird says   tikka-tikka
& one bird says   ka-kakakak
& one bird speaks for us all & says   oh-man oh-man oh-man

Autumn
so the fish stocks swell   pushing through the evergreens
clogging gutters   filling lawns

Forty-nine people shot & killed   so in spring the town is filled
with an uneasy Hanami   Check out the way
the ghosts emerge like bastards from the bush

& one bird says   soon-soon
& one bird says   and-then-some
& one bird speaks for us all & says   wow-okay wow-okay wow-okay

9

. . . heritage

Sad rose & tangled fuchsia
I think about the garden but
I'm no gardener
I'm a killer
like my mother
When she was looking for a house she said
I do not require a garden
I do not require the pressure &
stress & mess & skill of a garden
She's from New York
She required concrete
She found her concrete
in Newtown
& one day a pumpkin grew
right out of her concrete
Someone had dropped a seed &
here was this gorgeous pumpkin
She's so proud
She takes photos
She made soup
Plants herbs
to taste

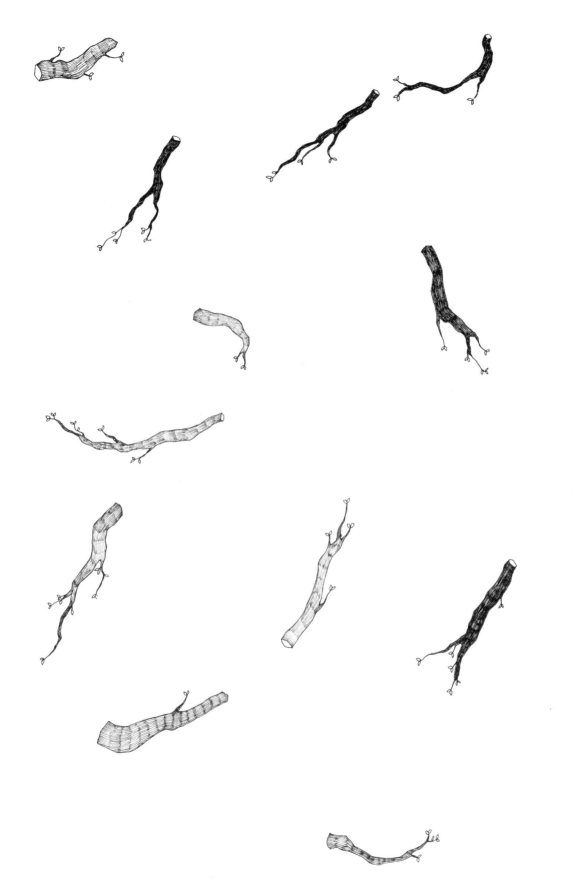

I'm Saying Kill 'Em All

I'm saying they came inside
                              because it rained all summer
I'm saying I see them dash in pairs

                              to some back-of-the-stereo party
I'm saying I guess they're sweet on Elvis
                              and for some reason this makes sense

I'm saying this makes sense
                              and endears them to me briefly
I'm saying I hear their gangbang sessions

                              afterwards in the ceiling
I'm saying I see them saunter
                              past post-coitally towards the pantry

I'm saying as the landlord
                              I don't relish these encounters
I'm saying they get into my bag drawer

                              and shit all over my spice rack
I'm saying I had to get all new spices   got traps
                              and the buggers ate the butter

with one gnarly foot on the trigger
                              Clever fuckers   but I've read Mrs Frisby
so I'm saying

                              I shouldn't be surprised

Daffodil Day

& motocross   starting at 10am
gumbooted crowds thread through the pines   Craig is coming
& Shayla   smell of sausage sizzle   bouquet   sound of
aerial warfare   drifting   'cross the yellow paddocks
                              Go for the buds   my babies
to count on longer-lasting displays   says the whaea to her flock
& the warblers   up their trilling   saying   *the old guard is still relevant!*
oh but they're obsolete   & they know it   cos   what's the point
of singing when it's   engines
that fill the valley now   & we love it ok & it's   rousing   like
this isn't a walled English garden   this is ten k's east of Carterton
this   is the sound of spring

Small body seeking   flirty frills   shy in   puritanical bonnets
& Smith is coming round the bend & he's gone & that's   gotta hurt
Small body twirls from stem to stem &   crouches in the flowers   like
pussycat   like   boy &   this event is   brought to you by
Mitre 10   the Masterton   Charitable Trust &   Ken's
Liquor Emporium   It's
a painting by a Dutchman with   a soundtrack from Metallica
casting by Frank Oz   It's   September   in the Wairarapa

Years Passed, Just Like That

he said   hi winter flower

she said   hi burned-out tōtara

he said   hi borrowed rifle   cocked

she said   hi city-slicker

he said   ok   little lady

she said   no   I have retired

he said   ok then   old fellah

she said   truth   it comes like a   reckoning

he said   it comes like a bullet   shaped   cloud in the spring

she said   it waits like the stock trucks   spattered idling

he said   oh   oracle

she said   goodbye glass box

he said   you're observant   that's all I mean

she said   well I saw you mowed the berm

he said   sometimes   I play along

she said   ok   self-styled village prince

                put your boots on and   play along

They both turn now to watch the trucks   hauling lambs uphill

While in the east

spring winds hurl   sound of *hoooooves*   up   the valley

Onwards and Upwards

How does it feel not to go up to M?

Feels pretty good not to go up to M

When I get in the car & remember   that I don't have to go up to M
that I don't have to deaden my eye up in M   stash my laugh or
mash my word up in M   I get all   glossy optimistic!
with fresh-linened smooth-legged relief!   saucy-eyed so energised
I swear I'd eat an apple!   if you had one!   feeling frisky
in the driver's seat up for sex!   or marathons!   dude
I'll run the whole sweet way!   smiling broadly like a leaf!
. . . such is the useful richness   of the relief that sears & flushes . . .
of getting in the car & knowing   that I don't have to go up to M

        Do you know what I mean? Do you know what I mean?
        Have you ever had to go up to M?   I got a handjob

from an old man   on a beach   in a posh part of Auckland
I hated living in Auckland too   but at least I got a handjob

Three days a week for   almost three years I was
going up to M   & I never got a handjob there

Souvenir

protest as much as you like old bud
                    there's a   rural   tang
that now sits in your gums

& maybe it's also true   that music
from the oily racer scum across the street
            is really the sound of a heart

pumping up in my ear

On Intimacy

Before

when I used to go round with the ocean   late night hook-ups
drunken punch-ups   surprising me with a present   in love again
the next morning   tantrums   frightening sometimes   I remember
but I like to be pinned down   don't you like to be pinned down?

The day before my thirtieth   I hooked up with a mountain & the
mountain took it seriously   now I'm married to the mountain   &
that's a domination . . .   of a different colour   in the winter
I spend baggy hours   paleing   in   his   shadow

I did get away for a day last week to south of Awakina   the ocean
puffed his savoury chest   we wrestled saucily till dusk   went to bed
with slap marks all over &   kisses in my eyebrows . . .

Old mountain   he knows   he's a mensch   cuckold   he's old   he
does his best   so   I guess   I'll hang around   plus
he's introduced me to this river   his mate   who is beautiful &
focussed   driven   interested in the world   affectionate but
with seasonal temper & on the same page as me more or less when it
comes to a   coastal urge

                           Meanwhile   all my friends are
pregnant &   getting   divorced &   dying
I'll stick with this mountain till Christmas   by then all the
ceremonies will be done &   stale pledges nullified   see me flicking
through my contacts   got my eye on you   Puponga

Untitled

Autumn now   so rivers glow   leisurely as a nap   Sun
hunched to pick   surveyor-like   along the black hill nape

I went up black hills & found   sad grey branches there
I went up black hills & found new branches that don't know anything

No name   came   caught me
in my bathrobe cleaning windows   I've been here almost five years
& I've never cleaned the windows   then
no name   came & there I was   up a ladder   cleaning windows

No name   is uptown   It's a beautiful ride
but it's old   I ride sometimes & feel   old

        float
            down

          freckled
    leaf

No name   turned in bed & said
    I dreamed of missing parties

To   no name   I turned & said
    you make me feel old and beautiful

An Ending

Drew a perfect line

sighing shoulder

mountain saddle

it was lovely

it existed

for a day

I took no photo

Poem About Love

The boy's in bed   he snores oh my god
the intimacy of   real muscle that laughs
          When a motorbike snarled across dunes
          we both wished the rider drowned in lagoons
          and that's love!   as far as I know it

Now I'm up with the spur-winged plover
to meditate over shared air   *new thing   touch*   and the mess of it
How fast   last night's sweaty grin   can turn of a beach weekend
          . . . cocooned afternoons of
          . . . cata   loguing   each   other's   scars
          . . . lightly pressing fingers against them
                                        feeling them buck or dissolve

Till I became crowded   slept   enraged and crowded
In the evenings   I took long strides around the house that meant
nothing and it all   Then woke up early
to the misty paddock gunning of spur-winged plovers

Hey   good morning   and forgive me I guess

          I'm no sure-bet paradise drake
          I slink solo around marshes
          a bittern in silk shoes   stabbing frogs and staying mute
          a bittern in a grass shirt   standing still and staying mute
          when a bittern decides to bolt   his wings

          are borrowed from a peregrine

Motorbikes on the Beach

May saltwater rust their bodies
May sand clog their fuel lines

May seaweed lubricate their paths
so they skid into the driftwood belt
to be flung like sticks for dogs

When the Romans trashed the Temple in Jerusalem   ran pigs
put out the Eternal Light   The clean-up was a daunting task
but someone sourced a little oil and now   we celebrate Chanukah

Just saying
mind your manners in church
The Roman Empire fell hard

Regeneration

when I was a child
I played by myself in a
corner of the schoolyard
—F.O.

The animals weren't friendly   but I insisted
& they became cordial   & if anybody asked   I'd tell them from
my place   in the eucalypt or oak   that I was a conservationist
The proof being my solitude & solitude's soiled knee   Soiled
for purity of intention & a gold star for dedication   Dedication
being measurable by the   years & the years that follow & the desire
to look up & see   more than a mean sun or blue
To look up & see   proof   of the epiphytic canopy I believed in

Now here I am   the centre of all   bucolia   making a sorry buck
where the catch cry is   *pittosporum*
When did trees get so   boring?   This is my pose   I hardly visit
anymore   I pose   like   it's   someone else's painting
of just so much windburned cheek

I got lost I guess   bad age
I know too many policy analysts & too few self-employed anarchists
or anyone   with a free afternoon   I'd like to fall in love
with a man who knows the names of trees   some Bruce or Dave or
Hemi who says

ngaio   will hurt your liver &
rangiora   is bad for horses

rewarewa   started popping up about ten years ago   Diane said
what the hell is this   when one grew & blocked the view

           The neighbour chopped it down
           They were having an affair

kahikatea   butter box
torn stocking trunk of kōwhai
tawai   battered remains

When I was a child
hills were hot with gorse   I hid in pine forests   saved a blackbird

Now the view through the windshield   is as close as I get

But it's heartening

in this wretched valley   to see the new dank walls   rising up like a
beautiful threat   &   I'm kissing a man

who knows the names of birds   so that's a start

text message

The weekend was eventful
my mother took me to the movies
and I picked an enormous lemon

Notes

This book's epigraph (p. 9) is from Frank O'Hara's 'Meditations in an Emergency' (1957), in *The Collected Poems of Frank O'Hara*, edited by Donald Allen (Berkeley, CA: University of California Press, 1995), p. 197.

The line 'My heart's aflutter!' in '. . . *coda*' (p. 26) is the first line of Frank O'Hara's 'Mayakovsky' (1957), in *The Collected Poems*, p. 201.

In 'Speaking Diary' (p. 31), the line *'She changed her name to Deveraux'* is from 'Mothers' by David Trinidad, in *Dear Prudence: New and Selected Poems* (Turtle Point Press, 2011), p. 28.

The poem '. . . *press'* (p. 55) was curated from artist statements found in ceramic art exhibition catalogues.

'Kim Hill Interviews a Famous Artist' (p. 73) is transcribed and adapted from an RNZ interview with Max Gimblett.

In 'Lawns' 4 (p. 83), the poets referred to by initial are John Dickson, Jericho Brown, Mark Doty, Kate Camp, Walt Whitman, Mary Ruefle, Hinemoana Baker, Gregory O'Brien and Hannah Mettner.

The epigraph to 'Regeneration' (p. 103) is from Frank O'Hara's 'Autobiographia Literaria' (1949 or 1950), in *The Collected Poems*, p. 11.

All illustrations are by Sam Duckor-Jones.